THE WONDER OF PUPPIES

THE WONDER OF PUPPIES

FOG CITY PRESS

Published by Fog City Press,
a division of Weldon Owen Inc.
1045 Sansome Street
San Francisco, CA 94111 USA

www.weldonowen.com

weldon**owen**

President & Publisher Roger Shaw
Associate Publisher Mariah Bear
SVP, Sales & Marketing Amy Kaneko
Finance Manager Philip Paulick
Editor Bridget Fitzgerald
Creative Director Kelly Booth
Art Director Meghan Hildebrand
Senior Production Designer Rachel Lopez Metzger
Production Director Chris Hemesath
Associate Production Director Michelle Duggan
Director of Enterprise Systems Shawn Macey
Imaging Manager Don Hill

Library of Congress Control Number on file with the publisher.

ISBN 13: 978-1-68188-095-2
ISBN 10: 1-68188-095-4

10 9 8 7 6 5 4

2017 2018 2019

Printed by 1010 Printing in China.

Puppies come in many different shapes and sizes. You see them almost everywhere you see people—in houses and cars, in the park, and walking down the street.

Puppies are great friends and have become part of our way of life. Every year, more people are bringing home pet puppies!

Puppies are born with their eyes and ears shut. They don't open them until they are two weeks old.

Fun Fact

A group of puppies born together is called a litter.

Fun Fact

Some litters can have as many as twelve puppies-or more!

Before they are even six months old, puppies will learn a lot. Like how to make friends—with each other, and with you!

Fun Fact

A puppy's nose print is as unique as a human's fingerprint.

Puppies can have long hair or
short hair. Some have spots.
Some have big floppy ears.

They can be
white, black,
brown, or gold.
Different breeds
have different
characteristics.

Fun Fact

Pug puppies have flat, squashed-looking faces!

Fun Fact

Jack Russells love to run and need plenty of exercise!

Puppies have very sensitive ears and noses. A puppy can hear and smell much better than a person.

For a puppy, every time is naptime. A puppy can spend up to twenty hours a day sleeping!

Fun Fact

A sleeping puppy will twitch and move while he dreams.

Fun Fact
Puppies don't have any teeth when they're born!

Puppies love to chew on toys, like sticks or bones . . .

. . . or even your foot!

Fun Fact

Puppies have almost twice as many taste buds as humans!

Puppies love to run around. They run so much that they use up twice as much energy as grown-up dogs.

Fun Fact

A puppy won't try to walk until about two weeks old.

Fun Fact

Puppies with large paws often grow into big, burly adult dogs!

Puppies love long walks, too. Spending time outdoors gives them a chance to exercise and learn about the world around them.

Fun Fact

A panting dog can take 300-400 breaths every minute!

When puppies let their mouths hang open and pant, they are using their tongues to cool off.

When puppies grow up, they can help people in a lot of different ways.

Fun Fact

Humans have kept dogs as pets for over 12,000 years.

Fun Fact

Herding dogs can even try to nudge you into place!

Some puppies will grow up to be police dogs that help find missing people. Some will herd sheep.

Some puppies will train to be guide dogs, or to pull sleds over ice and snow.

Fun Fact

Guide dogs start their training very young— they have lots to learn.

But for now, there's
lots of fun to be had!

Fun Fact

A dog's sense of smell is 10,000 times better than yours!

Fun Fact

The world's smallest dog breed is the chihuahua.

Puppies explore every place they go . . .
and they are very good at finding new toys!

Fun Fact

Puppies can begin learning commands at eight weeks old.

Puppies can be
our best friends.
They can become
part of the family.

Taking care of puppies means giving them food and water, plus spending lots of time with them.

Fun Fact
Puppies like to eat
five small meals
every day.

It means talking to them, training them,
and playing games with them.

Fun Fact
Dogs chase their tails a lot—it's good exercise!

Fun Fact

The more you say a puppy's name, the faster she'll learn it!

There are more than 800 kinds of dogs. And all of them start as puppies!

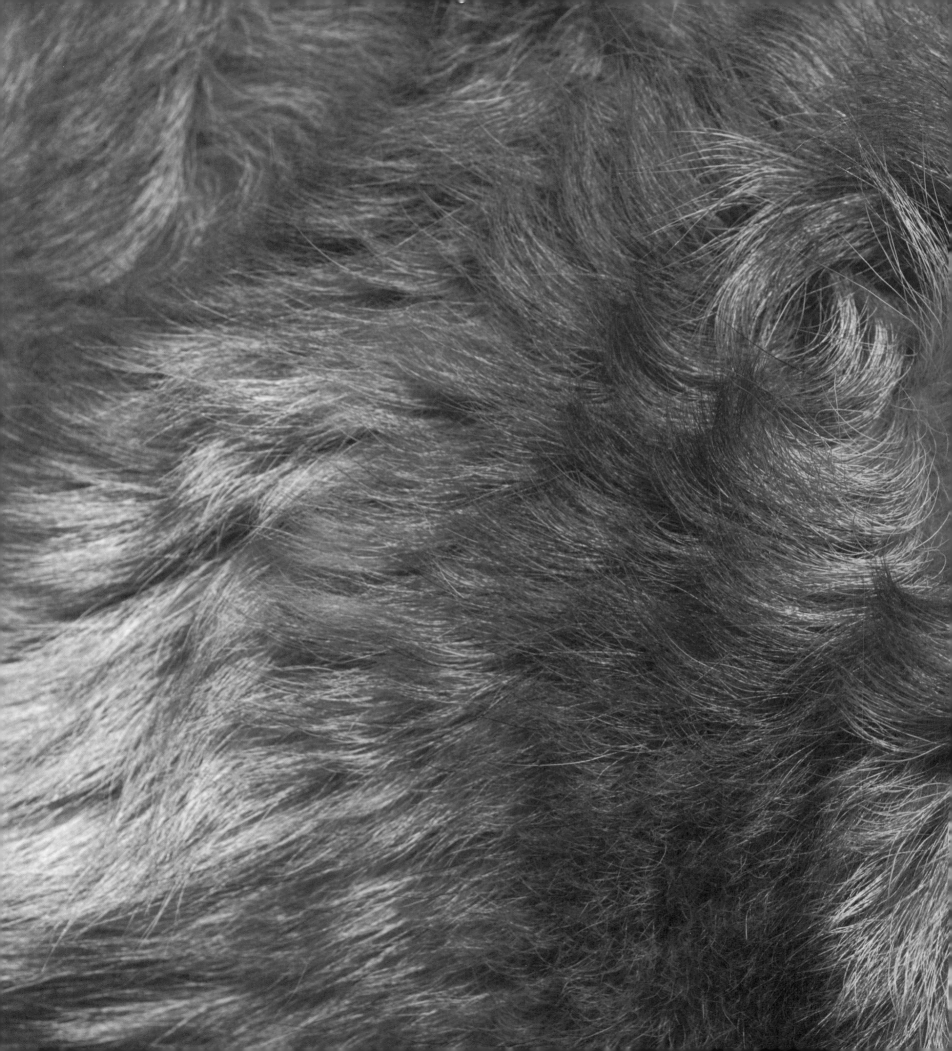